Homework !
Special Vowels

Abracadabra! You can add a light and happy touch to your child's learning time! *Homework Magic* will help you reinforce important basic phonics skills that will build the foundation for future learning. The one-on-one time you spend teaching your child is an irreplaceable gift that will give him or her the extra knowledge that will lead to self-confident, successful school years.

HOW TO USE THIS BOOK

- Choose a place to work with your child that is comfortable, cozy, and relatively free of distraction. This is special time!

- Remove the "magic wand" from the binding of the book. Tear the perforated lines to create the wand. Set the wand aside until it is time for your child to check his or her answers.

- Make sure your child understands the directions before beginning an activity.

- Invite your child to complete the problems on an activity page in pencil, offering as much help and encouragement as your child needs to feel successful.

- When it is time for your child to check his or her answers, show him or her how to use the wand to reveal the hidden answer. Have fun during this part of your learning time! When your child reveals the correct answer, say *abracadabra! or presto! or wow!* If your child reveals an answer that differs from his or hers... *Hocus pocus!* Just erase the incorrect answer and rework the problem with your child.

FS111117 Homework Magic—Special Vowels
All rights reserved—Printed in the U.S.A.
Copyright © 1999 Frank Schaffer Publications, Inc.
23740 Hawthorne Blvd., Torrance, CA 90505

ISBN #0-76820-431-3

Edited by Cindy Barden
Illustrated by Becky J. Radtke
Cover Design by Good Neighbor Press, Inc.

Let's Review!

Short Vowels

Print the missing short vowels in the blanks.

p__g

h__t

c__p

ch__ck

n__st

f__n

p__t

r__g

What do you get if you cross a bird with a small plate?

2

FS111117 Special Vowels

Let's Review

Long Vowels

Say the name of each picture. Circle the long vowel sound you hear in each word.

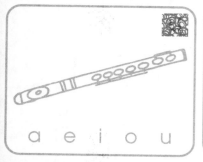

a e i o u

a e i o u

a e i o u

a e i o u

a e i o u

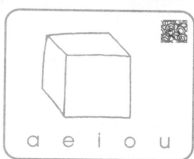

a e i o u

a e i o u

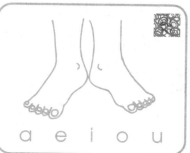

a e i o u

a e i o u

What has 100 legs, but cannot walk?

3

FS111117 Special Vowels

That Takes the Cake!

Long a and Silent e

When there are two vowels in a short word, the first vowel is usually long and the second vowel is silent.

Say the name of each picture. Fill in the missing letters.

__ a __ e

__ a __ e

__ a __ e

__ a __ e

__ a __ e

__ a __ e

When does a boat show affection?

4

Say the name of each picture. Fill in the missing letters.

_ _ i _ e   _ _ i _ e   _ _ i _ e

_ _ i _ e   _ _ i _ e   _ _ i _ e

Why couldn't the flower ride its bike?

5

Roses and Hoses

Long o and Silent e

Say the name of each picture. Fill in the missing letters.

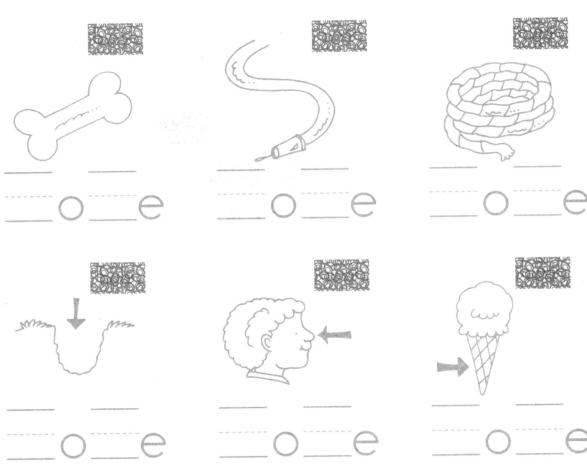

_ _ _ _ o _ e

_ _ _ _ o _ e

_ _ _ _ o _ e

_ _ _ _ o _ e

_ _ _ _ o _ e

_ _ _ _ o _ e

Why did cowboys in the Old West ride their horses to town?

Sing a Tune About June!

Long u and Silent e

Read each sentence. Circle the words with the long u vowel sound and silent e.

The mule will take June and Pam up the hill.

She has a cute pup on her lap.

The ice cube will melt fast in the cup.

Luke has a tube of paste.

Pam and Kate will sing a tune.

Write the circled words on the lines.

_____   _____   _____

_____   _____   _____

_____   _____   _____

_____

What did Paul Revere say to his horse at the end of his famous ride?

Rainy Day

Vowel Combination ai (rain)

*When **a** and **i** are together in a word,*
*they may have the sound of long **a**.*

Circle the word for each picture.

ran
rain
ray

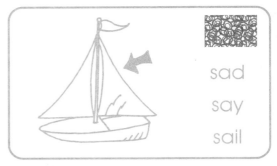

sad
say
sail

tan
tack
tail

nap
nail
nab

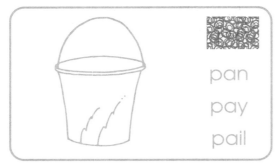

pan
pay
pail

plate
paint
pale

When is the mall like a boat?

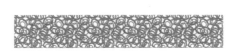

FS111117 Special Vowels

Today Is a Holiday!

Vowel Combination ay (jay)

*When **a** and **y** are together in a word,
they have the sound of long **a**.*

**Read the sentences. Circle all the words with ay that have the sound of
long a. Write the words on the lines.**

When the sky turned gray, it began to rain.

May I feed some hay to the elephant?

Today is a holiday.

Do you know the way to San Jose?

ay words

_____ _____ _____

_____ _____ _____

_____ _____ _____

_____ _____ _____

*What do you call a train
chewing gum?*

Birds of a Feather

Vowel Combination ea (bread)

*When **e** and **a** are together in a word,
they may have the sound of short **e**.*

**Use the words in the feather to complete
each sentence.**

feather   thread   bread
read   instead head

Yesterday, I _____ a book about a bird.

The bird lost a _____ .

A farmer wore it in the hat on his _____ .

He fed the bird some _____ crumbs.

*Why do birds fly south
for the winter?*

Thread the Needle

Vowel Combination ea (bread)

Use the words on the spool of thread to complete each sentence.

head	bread	thread
read	ready	feather

Dan will bake some _____ .

The class is _____ to go.

Pam had a hat on her _____ .

Last week I _____ a book.

I need some _____ to mend my coat.

What should you do if 37 frogs are on the back window of your car?

11 FS111117 Special Vowels

The Boat Floats!

Vowel Combination oa (boat)

Print the word that names each picture.

cook coach	soap soup	rock road

toad tool	too toast	bump boat

goat game	left loaf	coat come

 *Where does a seasick ship go?*

The Bee's Knees!

Vowel Combinations ea and ee (feet)

*When **e** and **a** or **e** and **e** are together in a
word, they may have the sound of long **e**.*

Print the word for each picture. Use the words in the box below.

leaf	bee	bean
feet	beak	seal

_____

- - - - - - - - - - - - -

_____

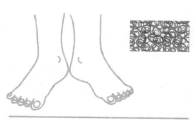

_____

- - - - - - - - - - - - -

_____

*What kind of umbrella does the President carry
when he goes for a walk on a rainy day?*

13 FS111117 Special Vowels

Match Up

Review ai, ea, ee, and oa

Match each word to its picture. Underline the two vowels in each word.

pail

tree

chain

boat

train

sheep

goat

rain

coat

soap

seal

stream

How do trains hear?

It's Cool at the Zoo!

Vowel Combination oo (zoo)

*When **o** and **o** are together in a word,
they may sound like the **oo** in zoo.*

Finish Joni's letter. Choose the best word to fill in each blank.

Last week our class visited a _____ .

zoo   zoom

We got there just before _____ .

room   noon

I saw some lions staying _____
inside their cave.

roof   cool

Later I watched the seals go swimming in

their _____ .

pool   fool

What kind of bus do
fleas ride on?

Toot! Toot!
Vowel Combination oo (zoo)

Write the correct word in each train car.

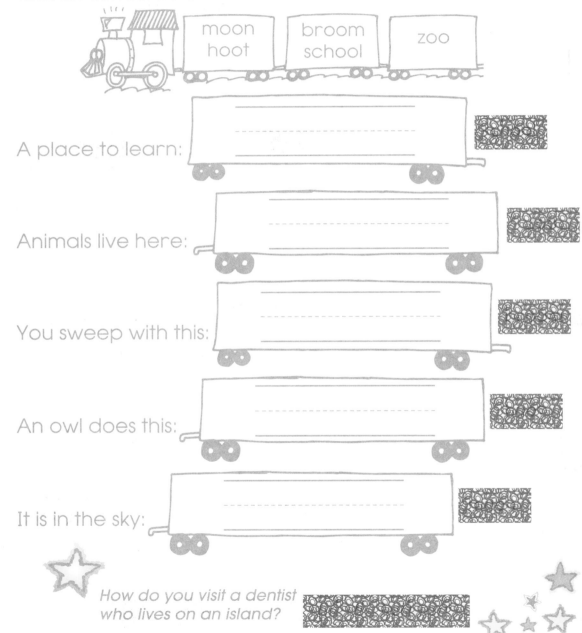

moon
hoot

broom
school

zoo

A place to learn: _____

Animals live here: _____

You sweep with this: _____

An owl does this: _____

It is in the sky: _____

How do you visit a dentist who lives on an island?

FS111117 Special Vowels

Read a Good Book
Vowel Combination oo (book)

*When **o** and **o** are together in a word,
they may sound like **oo** in book.*

Use the words in the Word Box to fill in the blanks.

Word Box

cookies   book   cooked   stood   woods   good

David read a funny _____ .

Terry baked some _____ .

Marc went hiking in the _____ .

Lana _____ on the hill and flew a kite.

Shawn had a _____ time at the circus.

Roger _____ dinner for his family.

*How does a sick pig
get to the hospital?*

A Moose on the Loose

Review Vowel Combination oo

Circle the word for each picture.
Color the pictures.

look

took

book

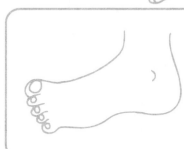

foot

food

hood

moo

moon

noon

cook

hook

hoof

moose

loose

goose

spoon

spool

stool

 What do old cars and babies have in common?

18

FS111117 Special Vowels

Double o's Are Cool!

Vowel Combination oo (zoo or book)

hook

book

wood

pool

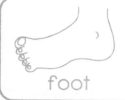
foot

spoon

goose

broom

Write the words with oo as in moon

_____

_____

_____

_____

Write the words with oo as in cook

_____

_____

_____

_____

What happens to illegally parked frogs?

FS111117 Special Vowels

Neigh! Neigh!

Vowel Combination ei (eight)

*When **e** and **i** are together in a word,
they have the sound of long **a**.*

Choose the best word to complete each sentence.

| eight   weight   reindeer   freight |

_____

A _____ is an animal with antlers.

_____

The puppy's _____ was seven pounds.

_____

A _____ train carries many heavy loads.

_____

Sonya has _____ brothers and sisters.

How do you stop a baby alien from crying?

My, My!
Y as a Vowel

*Sometimes **y** is a vowel. When there are no other vowels in a word, **y** is always a vowel. When **y** is the only vowel, it usually sounds like long **i**.*

Read the words in the engine. Write the words in the train car that have a long i sound.

my	may	you
try	bay	by
day	cry	baby
dry	say	yes

What's another name for the life story of a car?

FS111117 Special Vowels

It's Pretty Windy in the City!

Y as a Vowel

*When **y** is the last letter of a two-syllable word,*
*it is usually a vowel and sounds like long **e**.*

Read the words in the truck. Print the words that have a y at the end of the word.

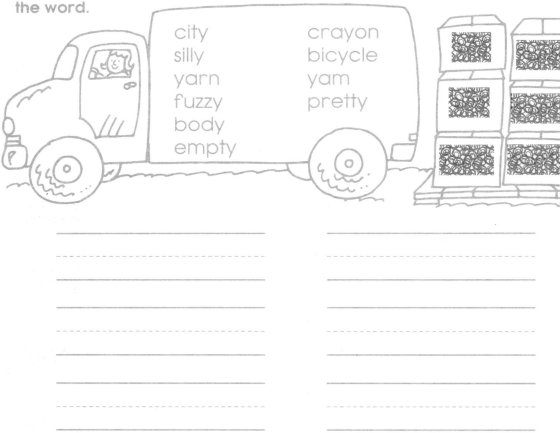

city
silly
yarn
fuzzy
body
empty

crayon
bicycle
yam
pretty

_____

_____

_____

_____

_____

_____

_____

_____

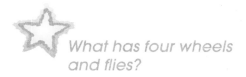

What has four wheels and flies?

A Sunny Sky

Y as a Vowel

bunny

cry

baby

penny

fry

sunny

sky

fly

Write the words with y as in funny

Write the words with y as in my

What does a bunny fly in?

FS111117 Special Vowels

Draw Straws

Vowel Combination aw (draw)

Look at the first word in each row. Follow the word pattern and fill in the missing letters.

raw   str_____

bawl   cr_____

lawn   d_____

pawn   f_____

Complete the sentences using words from above.

You must get up at _____ to see the sunrise.

A _____ is a baby deer.

How do bees get to school?

Can You Draw an Automobile?

Vowel Combinations aw and au (draw, auto)

*When **au** or **aw** are together in a word, they may have the same sound as in **auto** and **draw**.*

Use the words in the box to fill in the blanks.

daughter   drawing   fawn   autumn   claws   author

1. A _____ is a baby deer.

2. Many leaves change color in _____.

3. Greg is _____ a picture.

4. Paul met the _____ of that book.

5. Mrs. Lee has a son and a _____.

6. A hawk is a bird with sharp _____.

What ten-letter word starts with G - A - S?

FS111117 Special Vowels

Paul's Riddles

Vowel Combinations aw and au (draw, auto)

Use the words on Paul's list to answer the riddles.

saw
paw
hawk
fawn
auto
straw
saucer

This cuts wood.

_____

- - - - - - - - - - - -

_____

This is a car.

_____

- - - - - - - - - - - -

_____

This is a dish.

_____

- - - - - - - - - - - -

_____

This is a cat's foot.

_____

- - - - - - - - - - - -

_____

This is a baby deer.

_____

- - - - - - - - - - - -

_____

This helps you drink.

_____

- - - - - - - - - - - -

_____

This is a bird.

_____

- - - - - - - - - - - -

_____

Why did the woman refuse to get a license for her dog?

FS111117 Special Vowels

Snowstorm

Vowel Combination ow (snow)

*When **o** and **w** are together in a word, they may have the sound of long **o**.*

Use the words in the box to fill in the blanks.

snowed	rainbow	blowing	know

I _____ it _____
will be hot this afternoon!

The wind was _____
hard all day.

It _____
two inches last night.

We saw a pretty _____
in the sky.

How did the rocket
lose its job? _____

FS111117 Special Vowels

Round and Round

Vowel Combination ou (cloud)

Look at the first word in each row. Follow the word pattern and fill in the missing letters.

loud   pr_____

count   am_____

house   m_____

round   p_____

Complete the sentences using words from above.

Jessica is _____ of her brother.

Trina can _____ a nail with a hammer.

What is the strongest bird?

28
FS111117 Special Vowels

Nature All Around

Vowel Combinations ou and ow (cloud, now)

*When **ou** or **ow** are together in a word, they may have the same sound as in **cloud** and **now**.*

Choose the best word to fill in each blank.

A large _____ sat on a tree branch.

owl   out

Pretty _____ grew near a pond.

frown   flowers

A little _____ ate some seeds.

mouse   mouth

Two frogs hopped along the _____ .

found   ground

A wolf _____ in the night.

how   howled

What kind of truck does a ballerina drive?

29

Flower Power!

Vowel Combination ow (snow, now)

Read each word below. Decide if the word has the *ow* sound as in **snow** or the *ow* sound as in **now**. Write the word on the correct list.

clown	flower	town	cow
grow	blow	slow	brown
owl	know	window	snow

now

_____

_____

_____

_____

_____

_____

snow

_____

_____

_____

_____

_____

_____

What kind of car did the wealthy cat drive?

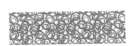

Read and Review

Vowel Combinations ou and ow

Write the correct word in each blank.

brown
mouse
owl

house
cow

1. It can squeak: _____

2. It gives milk: _____

3. It can fly: _____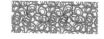

4. People live in it: _____

5. It is a color: _____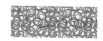

What was the first bus to cross the Atlantic Ocean?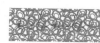

FS111117 Special Vowels

Join the Club
Vowel Combinations oi and oy (coin, boy)

Write the best word from the list to complete each sentence.

boy   Roy   enjoy   join

Would you like to _____ our club?

Do you _____ going for long bike rides?

_____ is the president of our club.

He is the only _____ in our club with red hair.

What would you call a bicycle covered with ice?

FS111117 Special Vowels

Oh, Boy—Toys!

Vowel Combinations oi and oy (coin, boy)

Fill in the blanks with oi or oy to make words.

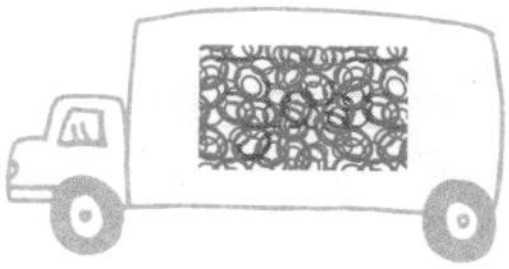

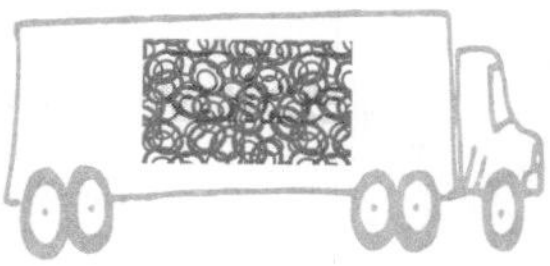

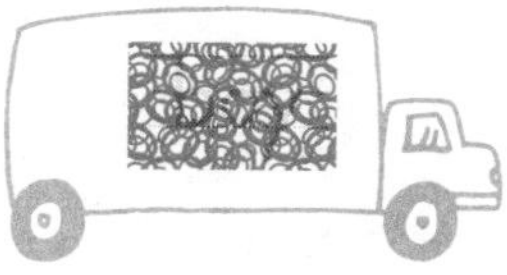

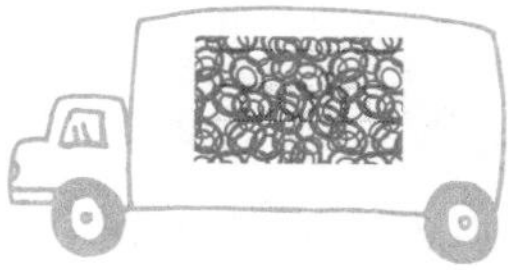

t _ _   j _ _ n   v _ _ ce

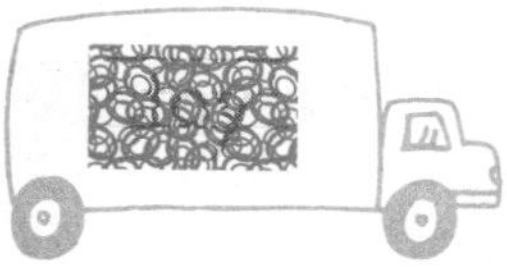

n _ _ se   b _ _   c _ _ n

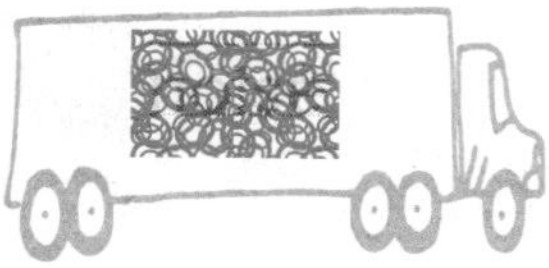

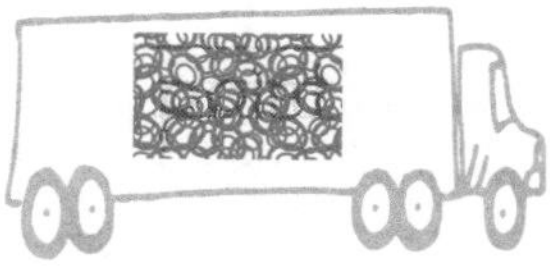

j _ _   p _ _ nt   s _ _ l

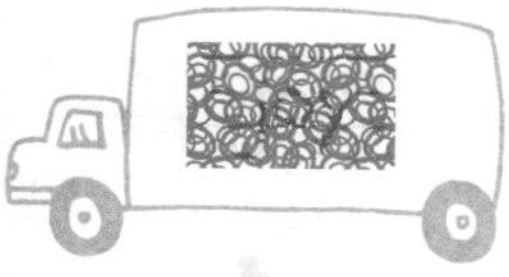

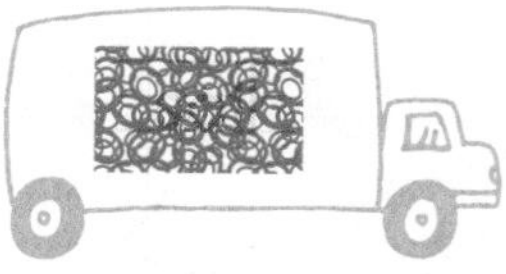

When is a car
not a car?

Sue's Glue Is New!

Vowel Combinations ue and ew (blue, new)

*When **ew** or **ue** are together in a word, they often have the sound of long **u**.*

Say the name of each picture. Circle the words in the box that have the same ending sound as the picture.

dew   chew
    were

few   threw

          owl

          screw

grew   draw

law   knew

well show
          flew

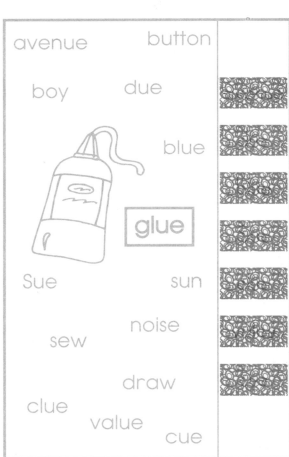

avenue   button

boy   due

             blue

          glue

Sue   sun

          noise
    sew

             draw
clue
    value
          cue

How many penguins does it take to fly an airplane?

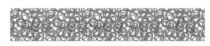

Write and Review

Vowel Combinations aw, oo, ou, oy, and ue

Write the correct vowel sound for each word. Use *aw*, *oo*, *ou*, *oy*, or *ue*.

m ___ se   c ___ k   g ___ l

h ___ k   b ___   c ___

What do you call a sleeping bull?

c ___   d ___ y   n ___

FS111117 Special Vowels

Down on the Farm
Vowel Combination ar (park)

Use the words on the barn to answer the riddles.

car   park
arm   barn
star

This is part of you. _____

This has four tires. _____

Farm animals can live here. _____

This is something in the sky. _____

Children can play here. _____

Why did the skeleton cross the road?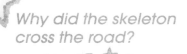

Pattern Parts
Vowel Combination ar (park)

Look at the first word in each row. Follow the word pattern and fill in the missing letters.

arm   f_____   h_____

bark   p_____   d_____

cart   d_____   p_____

card   l_____   h_____

What do you get when 5,000 giraffes try to get on the freeway at the same time?

37

Practice Patterns

Vowel Combination er (fern)

Look at the first word in each row. Follow the word pattern and fill in the missing letters.

fern   st_____

perk   c_____

verb   h_____

germ   t_____

Complete the sentences using words from the list.

They _____ late for school.

A _____ is an action word.

verb

were

Why did the man buy an elephant instead of a car?

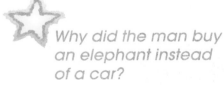

Swirl and Twirl

Look at the first word in each row. Follow the word pattern and fill in the missing letters.

fir   st _____

girl   tw _____

skirt   sh _____

bird   th _____

Complete the sentences using words from above.

Gina will _____ the batter before she bakes it.

Jose took _____ place at the track meet.

⭐ **What does it mean if you find four horseshoes?**

Honk a Horn!

Vowel Combination or (horn)

Look at the first word in each row. Follow the word pattern and fill in the missing letters.

born h_____   c_____

cork p_____   f_____

port f_____   sp_____

more c_____   st_____

Which side of an elephant is the most gray?

FS111117 Special Vowels

Stormy Morning!

Vowel Combination or (horn)

Circle the word for each picture. Color the pictures.

still   storm

stork   stamp

sports   spoons

tape   torn

corner   catch

fork   form

What does a car become after it's 50 years old?

Another Corny Riddle!

Vowel Combination or (horn)

Write the correct word to complete each sentence.

Let's eat some _____ .

horn   corn

Sam will shop at the _____ .

more   store

This coat is too _____ for me.

short   port

An ox has two _____ .

horse   horns

I was _____ in June.

born   torn

How can you tell which end of a worm is the front?

Order Up a Review

Vowel Combinations ar and or

Circle the word for each picture. Color the pictures.

cat

car

cord

jab

jar

jay

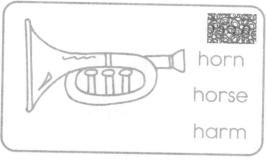

horn

horse

harm

for

far

fork

barn

bark

born

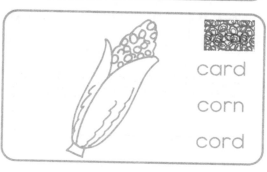

card

corn

cord

Why did the pioneers travel west in covered wagons?

It's Your Turn!

Vowel Combination ur (turn)

Look at the first word in each row. Follow the word pattern and fill in the missing letters.

purse   n_____

burn   ch_____

curly   b_____

curt   h_____

Complete the sentences using words from above.

Pioneers used a _____ to make butter.

The _____ gave everyone an eye exam.

What person drives his customers away and makes money at it?

Are You Ready to Review?

Vowel Combinations ar, or, and ur

Circle the word that has the same vowel sound as the picture.

Cows sleep in a .   her   hard   stir

Go to the .   mark   first   horse

Use my .   smart   port   hurry

I love .   for   start   dirt

Jam comes in a .   pork   art   her

Our  can swim.   barn   port   hurt

Did you cut your ?   turn   park   pork

 What did the traffic light say to the car?

Round-up

Vowel Combinations ar, ir, or, and ur

Read each clue. Find the answer in the list below. Write your answer on the line.

A food that is yellow: _____

Something you eat on Thanksgiving: _____

Something to wear: _____

The opposite of south: _____

A sound made by a dog: _____

Where to see a clown: _____

bark	turkey	corn
circus	north	shirt

What do you call a person who drives an ice-cream truck?

A Bird's-eye Review!

Vowel Combinations ar, er, ir, and or

Circle the word for each picture. Color the pictures.

bird
born
barn

far
farm
fork

car
card
cord

star
stir
store

ladder
letter
farmer

shirt
short
sharp

Why did the baby goose think a car was its mother?

Surprise!

Vowel Combinations ar, er, ir, or, and ur

Read each sentence. Choose the correct word and write it on the line.

Some cows live in a _____ .

barn   born   burn

I'm going to be in the _____ grade.

thorn   turn   third

If you don't _____ , we'll be late.

hurry   harry   hurt

At night, it is very _____ .

dart   dark   dirt

Take this pen and give it to _____ .

her   hare   hire

Meat from pigs is called _____ .

port   park   pork

What did the jack say to the car?

FS111117 Special Vowel